Copyright @ 2021 by John R. Brown and Brian J. Wright
ISBN: 978-1-5271-0700-7
Published by Christian Focus Publications Ltd
Geanies House, Fearn, Tain, Ross-shire IV20 1TW www.christianfocus.com

This edition published in 2021.
Reprinted in 2023 and 2025
Cover illustration and internal illustrations by Lisa Flanagan
Cover and internal design by Lisa Flanagan
Printed by Imprint in India

All rights reserved. No part of this publication may be reproduced, stored in a retrieval system, or transmitted, in any form, by any means, electronic, mechanical, photocopying, recording or otherwise without the prior permission of the publisher or a licence permitting restricted copying. In the U.K. such licences are issued by the Copyright Licensing Agency, 4 Battlebridge Lane, London, SE1 2HX. www.cla.co.uk

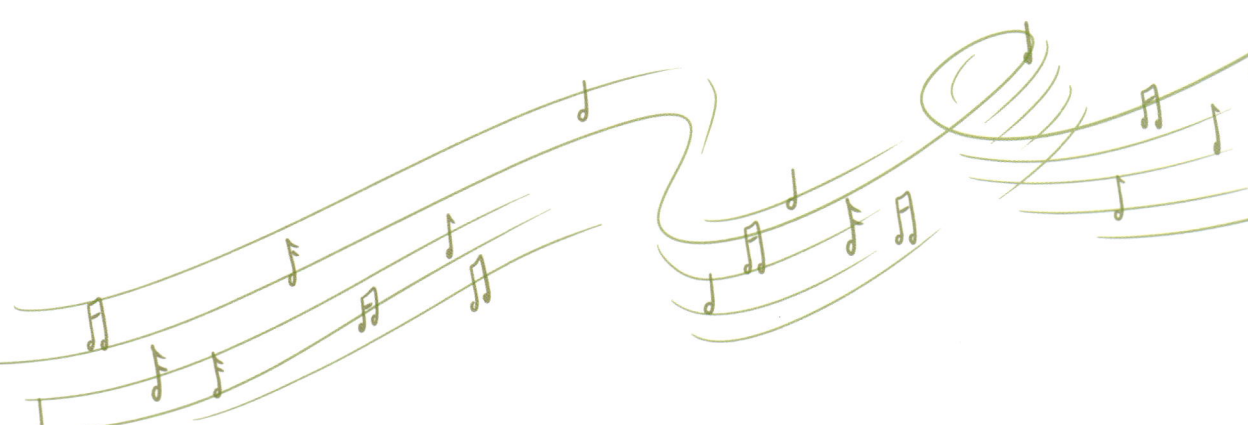

Habakkuk's Song

John Brown
Brian Wright

Long ago, **God's people Israel** were breaking God's rules.

God said, "Don't worship false gods." But they did.

God said, "Love one another." But they didn't.

God said, "Repent!" But they wouldn't.

This made **Habakkuk**, one of God's chosen prophets, really upset. He was so upset that he cried out to God.

"Help!"

"Bad people are hurting others everywhere! Aren't you going to do anything about it? Aren't you listening to me? How long are you going to let this go on?"

These were **bold questions!**

But did God get angry at Habakkuk? No, because he knew Habakkuk's heart. And God was about to do something about all the bad things mean people were doing.

"Look, Habakkuk, and be amazed!

I'm sending the Babylonians to punish Israel right now! They're coming faster than cheetahs, fiercer than wolves, like an eagle swooping down on its prey!" "They'll blow through the land like the wind and take my disobedient people away."

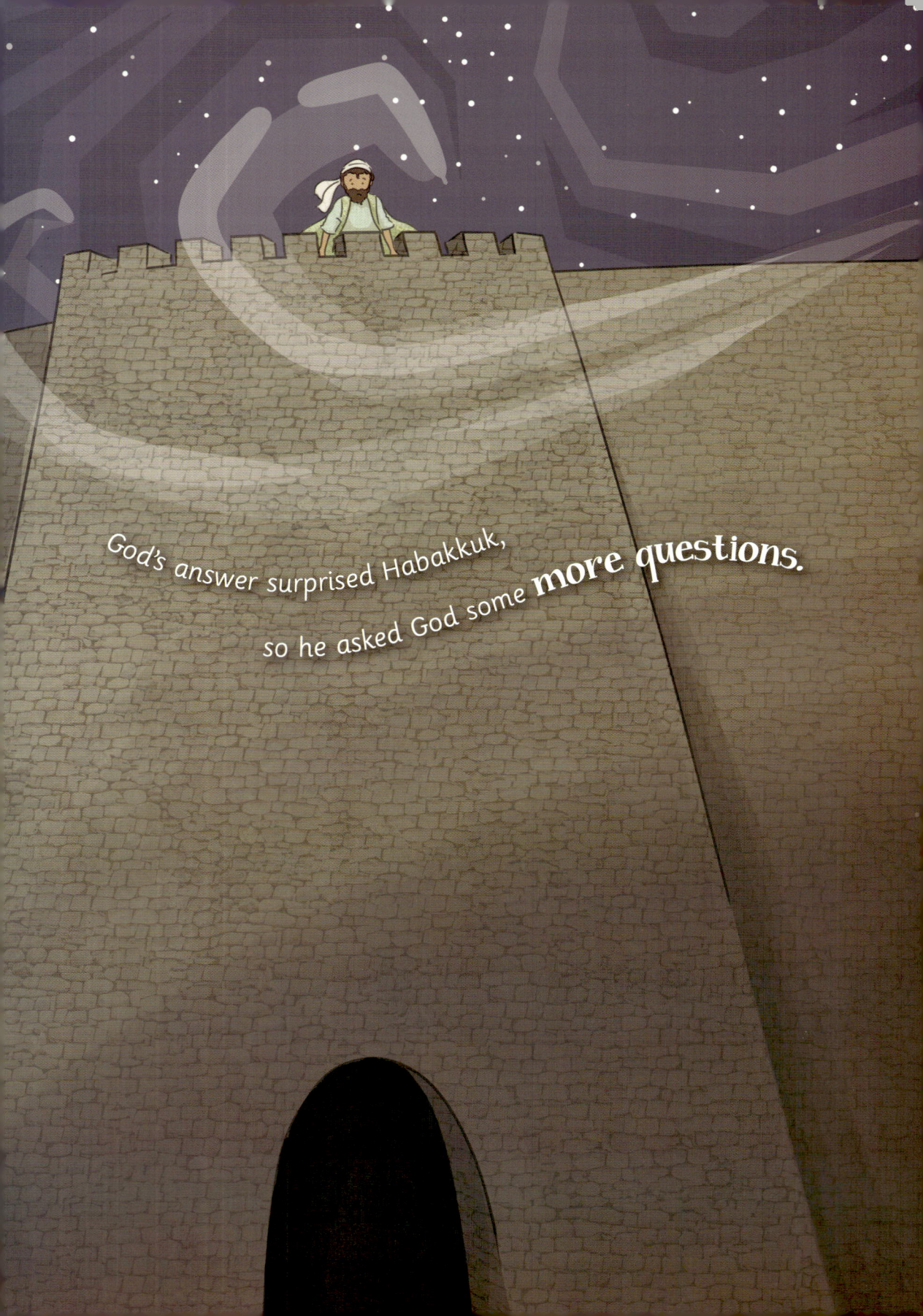

God's answer surprised Habakkuk, so he asked God some **more questions.**

"You are good, God.
Will you really let **these people**
do this to **your people**?

That's not fair! Won't you punish them, too?

Israel may be bad, but the Babylonians are worse!"

Then Habakkuk stood watchfully on the wall
to see what God would say.

"**Write this down** in your best handwriting," said the Lord, "so messengers can deliver my message on tablets for everyone to read."

"Someday I will punish selfish, greedy, and dishonest people. I will punish those who hurt others, who worship false gods, and who make others do bad things. Certainly, I will punish everyone who does bad."

"I will **punish** the arrogant Babylonians, who kidnapped their neighbors and stole their stuff."

"So **don't be like them!** People who are proud are wicked, but those who trust in the Lord are righteous."

Then **God** gave Habakkuk **five songs** warning how bad it would be for the Babylonians when God punished them.

"**How bad it will be** for you Babylonians, who hurt your neighbors and stole their stuff."

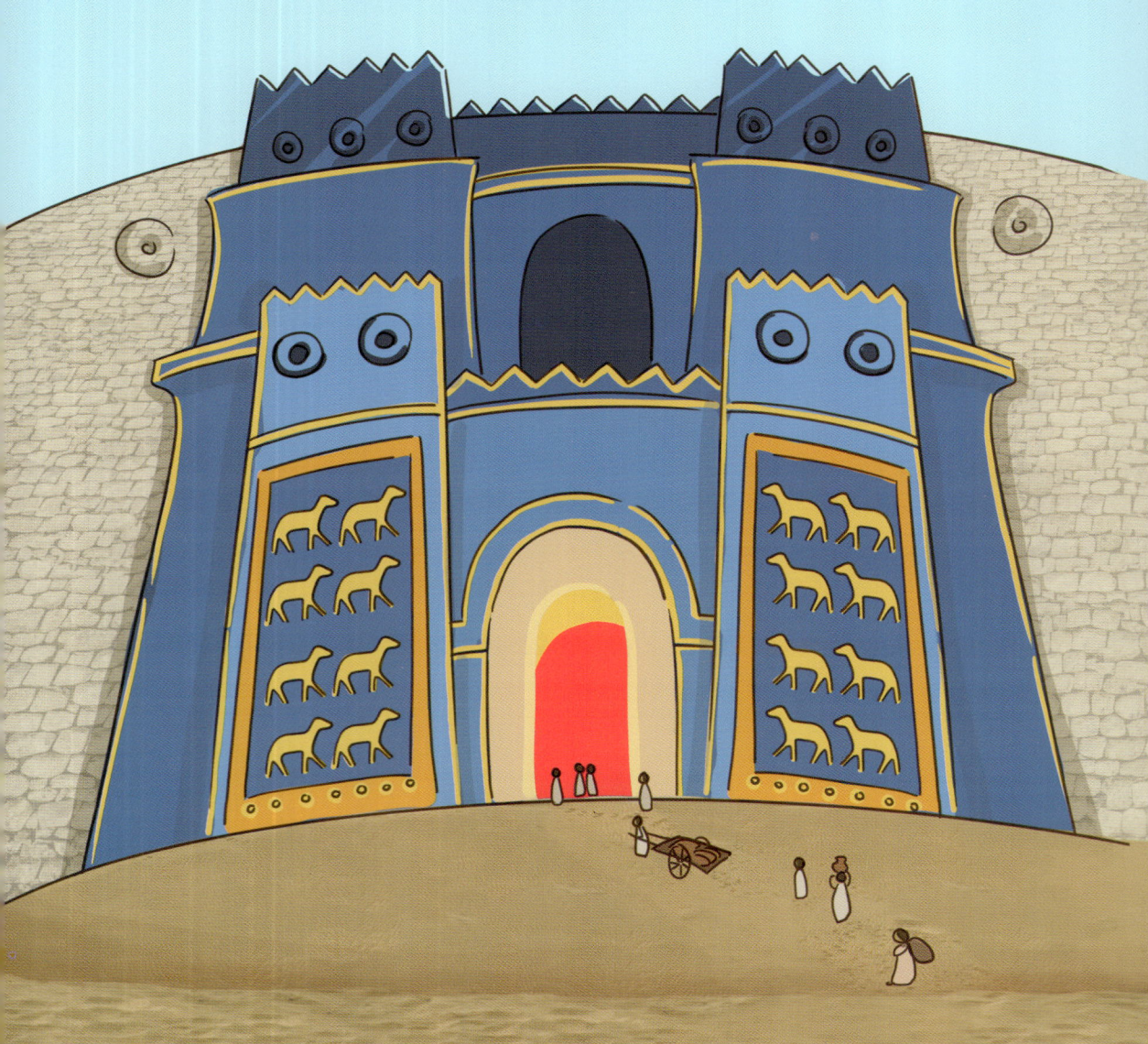

"How bad it will be for you Babylonians, who built your homes with money you stole from people you hurt!"

"How bad it will be for you Babylonians, who built your city with stolen money you got by violence! For God will burn your wicked cities down!"

"Indeed, **the Lord** will make all wicked nations like you disappear;
For **the whole earth** will know how great God is, like water covering the sea."

"How bad it will be for you Babylonians, who mistreat your neighbors and make them do bad things!"

God will punish them for everything! He'll make them drink **the cup of his wrath** down to the very last drop!

"**How bad it will be** for you Babylonians, who make idols that aren't alive and can't talk."

"**But the Lord** is alive, and he's in his holy temple, so let all the earth be quiet before him!"

After writing down God's five songs,
Habakkuk wrote **a song of his own.**

It was a song praising God for how wonderful he is
and for all he's done for his children.

"I've heard about you, Lord,

and am awed by all you **do.**

Please save us in our need,

and your mercy now **renew.**"

"I see God coming for us, like the rising of the **sun**. The mountains quake before him, for he is the Eternal **One!**"

"You rescued Israel from Egypt,

with your mighty chariots and **bow.**

And soon you'll crush your enemies,

just like you did **Pharaoh.**"

"You go forth to save Your people,

and your Anointed **One.**

For you crush the head of the wicked,

and victory is **won.**"

"Now I wait in frightened silence,

for the day you come to **judge.**

But even if all my blessings leave,

my joy in you won't **budge!**"

Our strength is still the Sovereign Lord, whose saving name we **hymn!** Righteous people trust Christ the Lord, and live by faith in **him.**

CHRISTIAN FOCUS IS FOR KIDS

That means you and your friends can all find a book to help you from the CF4KIDS range – from the very littlest baby to kids that are almost too old to be called a kid anymore.

We publish books that introduce you to the real Jesus, the truth of God's Word, and what that means for boys and girls of all ages.

Reading books is a fun way to find out what it is like to be a follower of Jesus Christ.

True stories, adventures, activity books, and devotions – they are all here for you and your family.

Christian Focus is part of the family of God. We aim to glorify Jesus and help you trust and follow Him.

Christian Focus Publications Ltd,
Geanies House, Fearn, Ross-shire, IV20 1TW,
Scotland, United Kingdom.
www.christianfocus.com

"Why do bad things happen? Habakkuk struggled to understand this – your kids will, too! With simply-stated biblical truths, Brian and John show us Habakkuk's trust in God and points us to Jesus who came to rescue us from a greater evil – our sin."
BARBARA REAOCH, former director of the Children's Division of Bible Study Fellowship International, and author of *A Better Than Anything Christmas* and *A Jesus Christmas*

"Too many people—kids and parents included—miss out on the rich truths of the Minor Prophets. I am happy to recommend Habakkuk by Dr. Wright and Pastor Brown as a rich resource for families. This fresh look at an overlooked book will bless you and your children."
DIANNE JAGO, mother of three, founder of *Deeply Rooted Magazine*, and author of *A Holy Pursuit: How the Gospel Frees Us to Follow and Lay Down Our Dreams*

"In teaching our children, Christian parents and children's workers are always on the lookout for expressions of biblical truth that are clear, simple, and understandable. They do so with hopes and prayers that, in using these, our children will see more of the beauty of God and his word as they understand these better. What a joy and blessing to have now a resource that does just this with one of the parts of the Bible that may seem most distant for our children, but parts that, rightly understood, are tremendously relevant and life-impacting. Brian Wright and John Brown provide beautifully crafted and compelling renditions of the Minor Prophets in ways that we and our children can understand better the powerful message of these books of the Bible. They carefully uncover the ancient context of these messages while bringing them forward to our day, and in ways our children can understand. I have no doubt of the tremendous benefit these will prove to be for countless Christian parents and churches."
BRUCE A. WARE, Professor of Christian Theology, Southern Seminary, Louisville, Kentucky, and author of *Big Truths for Young Hearts*

"The entire Bible, even the section called the Minor Prophets, is relevant for God's people, including children. Kudos to the authors for making the Minor Prophets accessible to children through these illustrated, engaging summaries of each of the twelve books. After reading these summaries, children should come away knowing what each book is about, as well as the important principles God wants us to learn. I'm looking forward to reading this book to my grandsons in the days ahead."
ROBERT CHISHOLM, Chair and Senior Professor of Old Testament Studies, Dallas Theological Seminary, and author of *Interpreting the Minor Prophets* and *Handbook on the Prophets*